I AM THAT
POET

JOSEPH LOWE

BALBOA.PRESS
A DIVISION OF HAY HOUSE

Balboa Press books may be ordered through booksellers or by contacting:

Balboa Press
A Division of Hay House
1663 Liberty Drive
Bloomington, IN 47403
www.balboapress.com
844-682-1282

Because of the dynamic nature of the Internet, any web addresses or links contained in this book may have changed since publication and may no longer be valid. The views expressed in this work are solely those of the author and do not necessarily reflect the views of the publisher, and the publisher hereby disclaims any responsibility for them.

The author of this book does not dispense medical advice or prescribe the use of any technique as a form of treatment for physical, emotional, or medical problems without the advice of a physician, either directly or indirectly. The intent of the author is only to offer information of a general nature to help you in your quest for emotional and spiritual well-being. In the event you use any of the information in this book for yourself, which is your constitutional right, the author and the publisher assume no responsibility for your actions.

Any people depicted in stock imagery provided by Getty Images are models, and such images are being used for illustrative purposes only.
Certain stock imagery © Getty Images.

Print information available on the last page.

ISBN: 978-1-9822-7468-9 (sc)
ISBN: 978-1-9822-7469-6 (e)

Library of Congress Control Number: 2021919935

Balboa Press rev. date: 10/20/2021

I am dedicating this book in memory of my parents, Dr. James Otis Lowe and Duree Price Lowe. My father earned a Doctor of Divinity Degree was a Minister and high school principal, which carried his last name, Lowe High School in Lee County, MS. My mother was a schoolteacher and an active member of the church and community. Being the ninth of eleven children, you both found the time to give me the love, attention, and the opportunity to find purpose in my life. Most of all, I thank you both for your prayers, for I know it was your prayers that kept me alive when I couldn't pray for myself. This book of poetry is dedicated to the memory of you two.

Your son, Joseph Theophilus Lowe a.k.a. Jim Dandy

CONTENTS

I AM THAT POET

When you are feeling low
and when your get up and go
have gotten up and gone
and you feel so all along
and as you read the word of my poems
may it make you feel good and strong
and make you laugh
at my jokes, or quotes
I want you to be able to say
that I am the poet, who once wrote
that he has been so low
that he could see eye to eye with a earth worm
but with faith and courage
he got back up
and when you need strength
to breaks your mental chain
you can remember one of my quote, or joke
that came from my brain
that made you get up, and not give up
I want you to say
that I am the poet, who once wrote

NEXT OF KIN

In life you had battles
some lost, some won
and you will encounter some storms
that's without a doubt
but before you began to fear
and began to pout
stick your lips back in
and pull up your chin
and give yourself a grin
and thank God, no one
had to call your next of kin

DON'T FEAR THE THUNDER

I hear the rumble of the thunder
and it put no fear in my heart
because I know, the rain that follow
will unfold the rose pedals in my yard
fear has no power once you know
that after the storm is over
that faith, love and courage is going to grow
and you will see the beauty of the rainbow
keeping on moving on
until you can't move no more, now go

KEEP SWINGING THAT MOP PEOPLES

Starting over is hard sometimes
and it can mess with your mind
but not impossible
if you don't let the habits. And failures
of your past mistakes stop you
this is what you can do
pick up the mop of faith
and put some love, faith and courage
in the mop bucket, of your heart
and began to swab
swab every corner of your mind
but don't forget about your soul to
do it with the faith
that have preserve all mankind
it worked for my mother, father, and ancestors to
you better believe it will work for you
if you want to do the do
that help you make it through
so keep swinging that mop
that cleans the spots
that only you knows
and the ones everyone knows about you to
just keep on swinging that mop of faith, love and courage
and cleaning those spots
until you feel and look brand new
stop hanging, and start swinging
and soon you be singing
a sweet tune, and dancing with the moon
if you keep swinging that mop

MY FRIEND WISDOM

knowledge made man aware, of his environment
but wisdom taught him to survive
you might have the courage, and knowledge
but without wisdom, it will be hard to stay alive
you would not be able to tell hot from cold
nor the different between a rabbit and a mole
you will mistake, your body for your soul
every poet is unique in his own way
I just keep it simple
and let the laughter flow
and share a little wisdom, as I go
if it add years to your life
and help you to meet your destiny
where wonders to unfold
may the words of my poems
not only brought you laughter, knowledge and wisdom
but a healthy, and brighter, wiser soul

I DARE YOU

I dare you, double dog dare you
to quit the stuff, that me you sick
the habits, the bad relationships
the sweets that makes your blood sugar go up
got you walking around, on shaky ground
like a volcano about to erupt
I dare you, double dog dare you
to stop drinking from that bitter cup
you already been up fool hill
why are you making another round
I am not telling you what to do
but you are the one is unhappy
looking sad and confuse, by the things you do
and giving excuse, why you do the things you do
that is destroying you, and everyone around you
listening to lies from, from your enemies
and people who use, and abuse you
Instead of the ones who cares and love you
and tell you the truth.
I dare you, double dog dare you
to brake the chains, that others have put around you
to keep you bound and on the ground
so they can use and abuse you
and after they get through, you have nothing to show
you're left with a closed door
I dare you to break free and be the best you can be
and experience the joy and freedom
who you suppose to be
you got a purpose
I DARE YOU, I DOUBLE DOG DARE YOU

CLEANSING TEARS

Tears that wash the windows of the soul
and stories of pain, that haven't been told
That have laid dominate since you were 5yrs old
It time to let the tears flow
to wash the pain, disappointments
and let them go, thru the cycle
and as your tears
fill up the washer of your soul
you can feel the churning of life up and downs
it is just the thing your soul have been through
it making the better you, and it just a cycle
and when your tears flow. In the rinsing cycle
it rinsing, all the pain and hurt dirt from your soul
and letting it go down the tide dee bowl
it was just a cycle
now here is the last one
that made your head spun
the spin that got your head going spinning around
but remember this is only a cycle
and you will calm down
after the spin cycle is through
and you find and clean and healthy soul
standing and looking back in the mirror
smiling, just grinning back at you

ANYHOW

knowledge made man aware, of his environment
but wisdom taught him how to survive
you might have the courage, and knowledge
but without wisdom, it will be hard to stay alive
you wouldn't be able to tell hot from cold
you could not tell the differents, between a rabbit and a mole
you will mistake your body for your soul
every poet is unique in his own way
just keep it simple and let the joy and laughter flow
just keep wisdom around you,
it will add years to your life
before they put that tag on your toe
just keep life plain and simple
and don't panic like a teenager
who has seen his or her first pimple
I am just a poet name joe, keeping it simple
I know I aint and I mean ain't a egar allen poe
enjoy this life, keep it simple
and keep moving on, singing your song
and don't worry about who did you wrong
just go on, just go on anyhow
but keep it simple, you will get your reward
and you can take your bow
knowing that you made it anyhow

DON'T CHEAT ON YOUR FUTURE

Don't cheat on your future, with your past
If your broken bones, have heal
why wear the cast
If you want to be yourself
you don't need no mask
pretending to be free
but still feel like a outcast
like a symphony, without woodwinds drums or brass
so get of your assets
and don't cheat on your future with your pass
because it's not what you say
but what you do, that going to last
you can't be free
if you haven't been harass
so do me, yourself, God, and everyone else
who is tired of hearing about your past
and get of your asset
and don't cheat on your future with your pass

WE ARE JUST PASSING THROUGH

From the dormitory rooms in the ivy league schools
to the housing project in every city.
There is a universal rule
we are not here forever
we are just passing through
you can't stop time
because you cry or whine
you can't stop time by what you do or don't
some people will, some people won't
it not what other think of you
but what you think of yourself
your hair will turn gray
if you live long enough
there will be aches and pain
and situations in this life
make you wonder, if you ever will get through
you can get peace, from the thought
troubles don't last always
so when headaches, peoples, situations, sickness come
and you don't know what to do
just remember, and find peace, and comfort in these words
troubles don't last always, it has a time limited
because we all just passing through

DROP THOSE STONES

If you have been throwing stones,
at other folks glass house
condemning them with your action
and also with your mouth
so when your glass began to shatter
and you wonder, what's the matter
did you forget that others have stones
to throw back at you, for the things you do
you better stop, and take stock
before you throw that rock
and remember you living in a glass house to
stop before someone break your glass
now you can laugh

DROWNING

I am not going to drown today
no matter what the weather, news
or what the doctors say
I have the life jacket of faith
tied around my mind, and my heart
to keep my from drowning,
in my troubles today
so if you try to stop me
I am giving you a fair warning
you better get out my way
because I am not drowning today
I swam past the troubles of yesterday
got caught in the storms of today
and I didn't drown
had the wind knock out of my sail
to make all this words clear and simple
I have swam through hell
I got third degrees burns, but I didn't die
some days I laugh, some days I cried
I swam through it all
just to tell the world what not to try
I am going to swim toward my purpose
even if it come hell and high waters
I have my life jacket of faith on
and I ain't and I mean ain't
going to be doing no drowning today
no matter what comes my way
on the stormy seas of life,
I will swim, through the trouble and strife
yesterday is gone, and the future is far away
but one thing I am sure of
I am not drowning today

LOOK UP

Look up, get up. shape up
and stop drinking
from that bitter cup
let go of the past
you already knew
that relationship wasn't going to last
you knew they had issues
and now you break out the tissues
Instead of seeing reality
as it was meant to be
you painted a picture, of make believe
so now comb your hair
and buy a new track for your weave
and watch the men roll up their sleeve
when you put on that smile
that haven't been there for awhile
so look up. Get up, wake up
and don't you give up

PS; IT WONT; HURT TO GIVE UP THOSE PIES
YOU SEE I MADE YOU SMILE
WATCH THOSE SWEETS, YOU EAT

LANDED ON MY FEET

I have been in the clouds of depression
and I have suffer some defeat
I have been in tornadoes, of confusion in my mind
I have been so broke, I couldn't, pay attention
to many times to mention
So when trouble came by the double
and my world, seem so incomplete,
and in the cabinets, and fridge
there's no food to eat
my soul can feel relief, in knowing
that no matter, how hard, and what direction
the ills winds of life where blowing
I always landed on my feet
and now I no longer worry
how I am going to make ends meet
I can wake up in the morning,
and look in the mirror, with a smile
knowing that it might take a minute
Or it make take a while
Or how high I go, or how low
rain, sleet or snow, or how the wind blow
and put on the seatbelt, of faith, love, and courage
and relax my spirit, with the knowledge, and wisdom
that storms in life are gonna come
and some battles, in life I have won
and others I have felt defeat
But no matter the outcome
I didn't crash and burn
and I am thankful
that I always landed on my feet

Joseph T. Lowe
T=Theophilus

METHOD TO THE MADNESS

There is a method, to the madness
there is s reason for the happiness
and a reason for the sadness
so if today, your troubles
that you are going throught
are driving you mad
for tomorrow, you will be glad
for yesterday problems
that you didn't have
so when you going throught the fire
and your brain began to burn,
don't panic, just say this is a lesson
I had to learn
and believe that there
is a method to the madness
and keeping on moving on
throught the fire before you get severe burns
and cause your mind unrepairly mental harm
and please don't sit still and pout
and choke, on the smoke
from your past mistakes, and pass out
because you will get burn up
and that without a doubt
and some one will
have to come and sweep up
your ashes and take them out
so you better keeping on, keeping on
and give some one a shout
to help you put that fire out
THERE IS A METHOD TO THE MADNESS

RABBIT IN THE HAT

You tried to pull a rabbit out the hat
but when you pull your hand back
you had a snake in your hand
and you said, I will never try that again
even if your breakthrough and victories
lies in that hat, along with all your this, and that
but the thought of that serpent is holding your hand back
and you are afraid to get back on track
thinking the train is going to wreck again
you aren't thinking where you going
you're thinking where you been
shake that serpent from your hand
and be heal by the hour glass fill with hope and not sand
so get up, and stand up, and be that woman, or man
and try again, again and again
sooner or later you will win
and you will heal, from your ill
and start climbing back up the hill to success
when you let go of all that unnecessary mess
somebody help me this evening

SAILING ON LIFE SEAS

Transformation is a process, and there will be a test
of faith, courage, and integrity
the test is to make you strong
for when depression and loneliness comes along
when the ship of past mistakes,
come sailing alone, and stare you in the eye
don't climb aboard, and cry and lie
just salute them as they sail by
and disappear in the mist
thank them for the lessons, and throw them a kiss
and move on toward your destination
sailing thought the storms and the abliss
you have no need to worry about your ship or cargo
for if you have faith, love and courage and hope
your ship will stay afloat
as it sails the stormy seas of life
throught the pain, sickness and strife
to get to the shores of peace, and happiness, in this life
my you find peace in the islands of your mind
as it sail throught the sickness, and the oppression of mankind
doing the this era of yours and my time

ONE AND DONE

In this life there will be a test
of faith, courage, and integrity
those test are there for a reason
to get you throught tough seasons
of a trouble past, the present problems
that you now have, and the future ones to come
hope that you learn your lesson
throught every season of troubles
and they have become, one and done
keep moving on, keep moving on

SEE THE INVISIBLE

those who can see the invisible, and feel the wind
even if they can't see it, but believe it
can do the impossible, can come back from adversity
and taste victory, again, and again
the evidence is present. in many people lives
who have gone throught poverty, misery, and strife
and became successful, in this game we call life
people have survive without a husband or wife
but who have died, behind the lack of courage and hope to survive
still confuse on what path to take
still hurting on past mistakes
wanting to give up, thinking it's to late
can't get pass the hate
that has been pass down throught the years
that has been payed by blood sweat and tears
so what is yours and my excuse about giving up
staying year after year in that same old rut
this is not the time to sit down, and moan
this is the time to stand up, and go on
but you got to believe, you can see the invisible
so you can do the impossible
and inherit the wind of courage, and faith
to blow you to your destiny date

TEARS IN A BOTTLE

Save your tears in a bottle, they can be use to water
the seed of joy, or the seed of sorrow
only you know, what you want to grow
for your tomorrow, if you plant the seed of defeat
that is what you meet, and it will empty your soul
but if you have faith, love and courage
it will make you complete, and make you feel whole
and this old world, wouldn't feel so cold
and what once made you scared
have now made you bold
so save your tears in a bottle
some for joy, courage and faith
to grow hope in your soul

THE JOURNEY TO PEACE

THE PRESENCE OR PEACE IS A JOURNEY
GOD WILL PULL YOU OUT OF ANYTHING
THAT HINDERS YOUR GROWTH WITH HIM,
PEOPLE, PLACES, THINGS
THAT HAVE BETRAYED
YOUR INTELLECT
YOUR RESPECT
YOUR DIRECTION…

WHEN A MAN'S BACK IS AGAINST THE WALL
AND GOD BRINGS HIM OUT
HE IS LIKE A SLINGSHOT OF RIGHTEOUSNESS
COMING OUT OF THE POWER
OF GOD'S RIGHT ARM
KNOCKING OUT ALL OBSTACLES IN HIS WAY SO FAST
HE WON'T KNOW HOW HE GOT THERE…

BUT HE WILL KNOW
IT WASN'T SOMETHING HE DID ON HIS ON
AND COME TO THE REALIZATION…
THERE'S GOT TO BE A GOD SOMEWHERE
IF YOU'RE CONTENT WITH
POVERTY
DEPRESSION
ANXIETY
THEN YOU'RE INSULTING GOD,
THE GIVER
WHO HOLDS ALL RICHES

ASK AND IT SHALL BE GIVEN
KNOCK AND THE DOOR WILL OPEN
NOT COULD, WILL OPEN
AND THE SCALES BE REMOVED FROM YOUR EYES
SO YOU CAN SEE HIM
AND SEE HIS GREAT WORKS
DONE IN YOUR LIFE
EVEN WHEN YOU DIDN'T ASK

TRIALS AND TRIBULATIONS

for without trials, and tribulations
we wouldn't learn the lesson
needed to give us strength
to stand up and face the world
with courage, to gain the confident
needed to pursue or undo
the damage we have done
to our self and our love ones
so when your trials comes
and they will
just say they are transportation
to ride you up the hill
to where you will
find your opportunity, and peace of mind
waiting for you there
in the clear, and peaceful atmosphere
living without fear

TONS OF BRICKS

I was about to give up
I was about to quit
but I had a second thought
that hit me like a ton of brick
it was you have been broke
and you have been sick
you been up fool hill
and you been a clown
why go back up that same mountain
going around, by round
so why not try something new
that going to benefit some one else
and most of all you
so next time you get hit
by a tons of bricks
the only things you need to quit
is the people, places and things
that is hurting you
and remember the Shakespeare quote
to thine own self be true
PS; You may need a couple of Tylenol
for some thoughts, that hits
like a ton of bricks

WHAT YOU SPEAK

If you speak fear
you will feel it
if you speak patience
you will endure it
if you speak doubt
you will not get out
if you speak peace
the storms will cease
and you will experience
the calm after the storm
may you find peace
after the words of this poem

STILL IN THE PROCESS

If you see me, walking down the street
and my, worn out clothes aren't neat,
and the shoes on my feet,
have worn out heals
from walking from place to place
looking for a place to eat, or sleep
as you look at me, don't laugh and don't weep
save you tears and pity for some else
I am gone to be alright
I am still in process
so if you have lost your relationship
and you feel depressed
and you haven't comb your hair
in weeks and you look a mess
and your friend ask what wrong with you
tell them, that you just going through
that not to worry now
that you are still in process
that you are going home and come your hair
and put on make up, and a pretty dress
and forget about that mess
and say to yourself
I am just going through the process

IN THE MEANTIME

As you climb your mountains
smile an laught along the way
until you reach the peak you seek
enjoy the scenery and landscape along the way
while you wishing in the morning
for the evening to come
go on and enjoy the midday sun
the joy is not the finish line
but the excitement, in watching the run
So enjoy this journey,
and small victories along the way
for when,we come to the end
you wont; have any regrets
for not seeing, and trying and doing
and realizing, this journey
is only a temporary stay

CORNER OF THE EYE

some times people will look at you
from the corner of their eye
and wonder how you getting buy
to tell you the truth, tell them
I got by, by not telling you
because some would have cut me down
before I had grown
and sent a decoy
to destroy me
you can't tell everyone your plan
for some will come
with a jack hammer to disman
all your hope and dreams
so sometimes, it best to put
your dreams in a boat
and row quietly, and gently
down the stream

COOKING COURAGE

like the batter of bread that's uncooked
courage not applied
it's like a book cover
without the book
anyone can yell from the stand
and say you a lesser man
but didn't have the courage to do
what you did, to make it to the field
taking about how they can fight
but afraid to take up the sword, and shield
they say if you, have been delayed
it doesn't mean you haven't been denied
but it's hard to have good home cook courage
if it hasn't been tried, fried,
layed to the side, and dried, and applied
,

POETRY

poetry can open the door to darkness
or it can open the door to light
it all depends of the poet who write
you don't need a college degree
for poetry is free it's everywhere
it's in a newborn baby smile
it's in the loins eyes in the jungle wild
in the gray clouds
and the blue clouds too
in the midday sun
and the morning dew
it's in the rich man
and the homeless man too
it's in me, and in you
your life is the pen you write
you have a choice
to live in the darkness
or light, that your life write

RAIN ON THE WINDSHIELD

There is rain on his windshield, and a pain in his heart
he won't go to the doctor
and he is afraid to go to the lord
stuck in the mist outside and in
darkest and confusion of the night, is his only friend
the liquor stores, and bars are close
and his so call woman, won't let him in
and he doesn't have any other shelter
than the car he is in
he has used and abuse all his friends
no one left to deceive, or tell lies to
everyone patience with him have worn thin
gas hand on empty, no driveway to drive in
all the years of his street life
have lead to a dead end.
this words I now write, may seem cruel
life is hell waking up as a 50yr old fool,
so tell all your nieces and nephews
that the years of alcohol, drugs, women and so call fun
have now led you to a life of a bum
that life has hurt you and made you say ouch
and that why you asking at 50yrs old to sleep on their couch
but their is hope for him yet
if he open up heart, and clean out his ears
he can enjoy time with family, and friends soberly
before his time disappears
and he don't have to down
only being a clown, who wouldn't put the bottle down
but a man who woke up as a 50yr old fool
and live to tell the story of grandma's rule
that said be a fool some of your life,
but not all your life

WOULD'VE COULD'VE SHOULD'VE

They say hindsight is twenty twenty
thinking you could've a dollar
but you didn't do the things
you should've done
and you end up with a penny
saying you could've been a doctor
or whatever you wanted to be
if you would've stayed in college
but instead of staying in class
and getting that knowledge
you were layed in bed
with a headache from the party
saying you should've
your relationship with that snake
after you put him, or her. in your arms
you need not feel so alarm, after you got bit
you knew they was a snake all along
so don't wait until your death bed
for your would've. could've should've
to visit you, laying there, and there ain't
and I meant ain't incorrect English
for all you English Teachers
nothing you can you can do
so began to live now, and enjoy
before your would've, could've should've
comes back to haunt you

LIFE WEATHER STATION

sometimes life will sent a tornado
to blow away things
that you couldn't let go
and don't need no more
that person you wish you never met
and cause a number ten earthquake
on the rectal scale of your life
you did not misread
and I did not misspelled
I am writing about
life weather that
somedays can be blue skys in heaven
or a volcano sent from hell
the weather in life could be your
boss, spouse your relationship
or the things you do
that is destroying you
that your, you know what
I am taking about, need to do
so you can't changes the weather
this is true, but you can
change the storm in your mind
by not during the stuff that destroying you
and bring in the sunshine, in your mind
by being, to thine own self be true
just stop lying to yourself, and those tornadoes
will stop spinning in your head
I hate to sound so cruel,
but if this is what it take, to get through
to you stop before you are dead
and walk in the sunshine, in your mind
before time, causes the sunset in your life

GO TO THE BACK

J. THEOPHILUS LOWE

An 18-yr-old U.S. Marine, stationed in the 2/9th
Batallion, Camp Swab, Okinawa JP, 1975

When I rode the bus in '63
There was no seat for me
They said, "Get your rags and sack,
And move on to the back.
You don't sit in front, just go to the back.
I was pushed to the back like cattle in a herd
Without hesitation, without a word
It was the same when I went to eat
They said, Get out with your nappy hair,
And no shoes on your feet
All your kind go to the back
And get your food in a sack
Don't you come to the front, you go to the back"
They called me "Boy" for seventeen years
But they call me a man when I get overseas
Shooting and killing for no reason I know
And after I return, still got nothing to show
so, when they said, "Go to the front of the line
With fifty pounds of gear on your back,
I told 'em, "No Thanks! I'd rather stay in the BACK",
Haven't you seen enough of my blood, sweat and tears
Left on the streets and in the cotton fields?

I would gladly go to the front and give my life
Knowing there's a future for my child and my wife
Knowing that my dying in this foreign land
will not be in vain
Knowing that I'm dying for a united cause
Not for one race, creed, or color

But for all

MISTAKES

If you not making mistakes
you are not making decisions
because they will be made
regardless of education, or religion
why get knock down
while you sitting down
at least stand up and face your fears
and if you get knock down
you can gain the strength
to fight another round
and get courage, for the battles to come
its not that you won't experience fear
but you will face them
you will stand up
and fight. And not run

PEELING BACK THE ONIONS

Sunday Sun

Peeling back the onions
will make you cry
but as each layer disappear
so will your fear
so keep peeling
and moving forward
as the tears continue to run
you will find, a peace of mind
as you leave your past behind
keep peeling, back, with the knife
of hope, faith and courage
and you will survive the storm
and when the morning come
you will feel, the warmth
and rays of the Sunday morning sun

WHERE THE MISFITS FITS

There is a place where the misfits, fits
and where the outcast laugh
you ask how can they celebrate there lots in life
without a get out of jail free card pass
I am not a poet, with a master, degree
I am a poet, of the ordinary peoples
who works, and those who walk the street
looking for a place to eat, of sleep
and the elite, who is looking for
a peace of mind, during our tying times
I offer faith, hope, and courage, in my rhymes
for no man, or women
no matter what title they hold in life
can hold the imagination captive
when it's want to be free
and for all the critics, of the world
for whoever they maybe
my pen will keep on writing,
my typewriter, will keep on typing
those words of hope, faith and courage
and give laughter, and peace to hurting souls
that want to be free, no matter,
who they maybe

BE THAT

Don't let your belief, about yourself
hold you back, with low self esteem
and the I can't, eating them up
as a mental snacks, feeding the negativity
and making it fat
while your positivity is getting lean
going out a playing in the dirt
while you hurting, to get clean
while you doing those negative things
feed your positive, and make it fat
and get the energy, to obtain the courage
and integrity to be that
be that what makes you happy
and make your eyes gleams
while you follow your dreams
and not do the things
with people, or places, or belief
that lower your self esteem
just stop what every is holding you back
start now doing, the things
that make your positivity fat
and go on, and be that

THAT STILL VOICE

He hears a still voice from within
that says you don't
have to stay in the shape you in
come to me my brother
for I am your friend
and will get you out of that hog pen
even thought you lost
your money, your car, your home
your family, your friends,
and everything you own
I got the grace, and mercy
and direction to help
you find your way back home
I have been with you all time
and most of the time
you paid me no mind
for I am the voice, of the good in you

Printed in the United States
by Baker & Taylor Publisher Services